Indian Poems

Indian Poems

by

Joseph Hart

© 2022 Joseph Hart. All rights reserved.
This material may not be reproduced in any form, published,
reprinted, recorded, performed, broadcast,
rewritten or redistributed without
the explicit permission of Joseph Hart.
All such actions are strictly prohibited by law.

Cover by Shay Culligan
Cover image by heylis

ISBN: 978-1-63980-092-6

Kelsay Books
502 South 1040 East, A-119
American Fork, Utah 84003
Kelsaybooks.com

—JKD

Acknowledgments

These poems were first published in Dr. Vivekanand Jha's journals, *Verbal Art and Phenomenal Literature*.

Contents

Lines	11
The Kitten	12
Legacy	13
Clouds	14
Keith	15
Somewhere a cat	16
Keats	17
The Biggest Question	18
11 Lines	19
Madness	20
While Looking at Bernini	21
Empty	22
The Future	23
ESP	24
Love	25
Compassion	26
My Last Duchess	27
What is Chartres?	28
Chaos	29
Dickinson	30
Proust	31
Prosody	32
Lines	33
A Cat's Tail	34

Lines

"God is love," the prophets said,
In spite of death and pain.
All life responds to love. Instead
The people go insane.

But animals will only live.
And Man is not above
Kittens who, although they give,
Don't make a God of love.

The Kitten

Tiny skull and spine
That curves into a tail -
Lying in the sun,
Fragile, small and pale -

Nothing else remains -
A kitten hardly grown -
Much can be inferred from this.
Nothing can be known.

Legacy

Intelligence has realized
Every human dream,
Intelligence that's far above
Predatory kings—

Kings that like a magnet draw
Ugliness from mobs,
Mobs that cannot understand
Or do what great men do—

But topple statues, smash the shrines
Or vomit in the temples -
Destroying art because it's art,
And good because it's good—

Clouds

Do animals see beauty in the clouds,
Rifts and puffs? Or beauty in the sea?
Heaven and eternity in shrouds?
Or genius in the instincts of a flea?

Keith

You don't remember Jacqui.
You do remember John.
Memories break up
Like cobwebs and are gone.

Less than nonexistent,
Elusive as today,
Tomorrow never comes
And yesterday won't stay.

Now I live alone
Throttled by a past
That everyone's forgotten;
Memories don't last.

Like a coral reef
Buried in the sea,
Ships continue passing,
And life is memory.

Somewhere a cat

Somewhere a cat
Rubs its side against a fence.
That's sleep.
Cobwebs across doorless jambs
Are doors.
That's the moon.
Dark purple wine
Splashes down the sides
Of a lead mug.
That's the night.

Keats

Like a silver star,
Junkets' verses sing,
Hanging in the cosmos,
Not attached to anything.

Neither are they personal
And neither history,
But cold and unapproachable
Perfect poetry.

The Biggest Question

Was I only born to live and die,
Then go into a grave and just decay?
Can this be all there is? It can't be. Can it?
Is consciousness the work of evolution?
Extending to the feelings of a cat?
And everything I think in opposition,
Nothing except fodder for a song?
Death is vanquished by the savior: love.
Perhaps. Except love doesn't come to all.

11 Lines

Art for art's sake. Everybody tries
To write it. Even me. The magic phrases—
Inspirations while I'm drinking coffee—
That artificial do not mean a thing.
Even Junkets didn't try to write them.
Sincerity, imagination, something
Flowing in a line across the page
That's beautiful with meaning. Can there be
Anything—like Shakespeare—that will show
The feelings and endure a century?
Not just a century; eternity.
A perfect union of the heart and mind.

Madness

You discover books and think
Reality is yours
And paradise, and then you learn
The writer you liked most
Went insane or shot himself.
Paradise collapses.
It was only words and feelings.
Words somehow made big
By genius or by madness.
What are words?

While Looking at Bernini

Maybe art's exhausted—
Like the dinosaurs, it's gone—
Sculptors and composers,
Painters, poets—gone.
Perhaps as things continue,
Some day further on
There'll be another Renaissance,
New Gods, another dawn.

Empty

To write about the people
I like to say I knew—
Who did I know? Any?
Except their hearts were true.

The singular fidelity
Discovered in a cat—
Or write about myself—
Do I know even that?

Or conjure up a mindless
Phrase about a tree—
Or compare a night of slumber
To a peaceful sea—

The Future

Hopefully to see
A resurrection of old times
When editors don't vomit
When they notice something rhymes.

And rhythm's not anathema
To poetasters hence.
And poems to be beautiful
Must at least make sense.

ESP

Suppose there were ghosts.
What would you say?
Summon a preacher
To drive them away?
Chase them from shadows?
Forbid them the day?

Suppose I read minds.
What would you do?
Suppose that your dreams
Told fortunes for you.
And all these predictions
Really came true.

Suppose there were things
That no one could see.
More things in heaven
Than in poetry.
Would they be good?
What good would they be?

Love

Stale beer and cheap motel rooms—
Winds that whistle silently
Through old ruins—

Breathless ghosts of people, thoughts
And feelings—love
That never was—is it
All illusion,
Guesses, hope
And fantasy?

Passing music that in time
Will be as common, unremembered
As the prehistoric night—

Compassion

Children are like cats.
Treat them any way you like,
They'll love you. If you're cruel,
In their minds,
They'll think you love them anyway.
Your check to immortality
Is a child's forgiveness.
Hell must be the absence of illusions.

My Last Duchess

There she sits. She's dead, you know.
Silent as a tomb.
We together pass our days
In this empty room.

She doesn't smile. She doesn't speak.
She doesn't walk or laugh.
That's what I want. My love song
Is an epitaph.

A marble sleep, shut eyes of wax;
I shall not marry thrice.
I murdered her. I did. Because
She was very nice.

What is Chartres?

What is Chartres? Is it a cathedral
Or the brief expression of a concept?
An old, abandon building is condemned.
On one crumbling wall I'll draw my face,
The dearest image and the oldest source,
A perfect likeness of mortality.

Chaos

"Guernica"! Christ! What can anyone do?
Think of solutions. Get out of the fire.
Madmen make nonsense of all that you knew
Was probable, right. Even God is for hire.

Science reveals that the earth is a freak.
Lovable babies, endearing and new,
Grow up to be bigots. And each time you speak,
A man with a purpose shoots bullets at you.

The people you love are as foreign to you
As sailors and Chinamen over the sea;
Strangers. You talk to them. Each time you do,
You're holding a riddle, slippery, free.

You have no effect. And it's useless to try.
Nothing's as sure as the love of a cat.
Life is a promise. You're starting to cry
In futility. Nothing's as futile as that.

Dickinson

Her melodies on God,
Clover bells and bees,
Heaven and eternity and birds—
All her tiny poems
On subjects such as these
Are precious—too much so
For clumsy words.

Proust

Enduring but forever,
With a steady hand and sure,
He made a perfect music out of noise.
Proust said that an artist
When he is mature
Will write about the things that he enjoys.

Prosody

Once when I was young—
I was once, was I not?—
Poetry and lyrics
Were my chosen lot.

What is verse? I wondered.
I thought and thought and thought
About it, and it seemed
It's rhythm, rhyme—and what?

Lines

My poems are a window on the night,
If the window's ice and night is empty.
I'd rather be Millay or Johnny Keats.
Who am I? Or what? Personify
Nothingness. And that is poetry.
Though not with the indifference of a tomb.

A Cat's Tail

Tread upon a cat's tail.
He will yelp and run away,
Then cower and look sad as if
He thinks he isn't loved.

Pet him for a moment. He will
Jump into your arms,
Seeming to be happy to
Believe he's loved again.

About the Author

I have a BA. I've had poems published in small magazines and was twice nominated for a Pushcart. Three collections of poems I wrote ("For Kitty", "Idle Fancies" and "An Empty, Abandoned House") were published by Cyberwit.net. My favorite poet is Keats.

www.ingramcontent.com/pod-product-compliance
Lightning Source LLC
Chambersburg PA
CBHW071642090426
42738CB00013B/3192